W9-DHI-263

UNDERSTANDING SOUND

Follow the Clues

by Tamra B. Orr

CHERRY LAKE PUBLISHING · ANN ARBOR, MICHIGAN

CHERRY LAKE
Publishing

Published in the United States of America by Cherry Lake Publishing
Ann Arbor, Michigan
www.cherrylakepublishing.com

CONTENT EDITOR: Robert Wolffe, EdD, Professor of Teacher Education, Bradley University, Peoria, Illinois

PHOTO CREDITS: Cover and page 1, ©Fort George G. Meade Public Affairs Office / tinyurl.com/ lxtyfnd / CC-BY-2.0; page 4, ©Jim West/Alamy; page 5, ©Piti Tan/Shutterstock; page 6, ©Hurst Photo/ Shutterstock; page 7, ©phomphan/Shutterstock; page 8, ©shipfactory/Shutterstock; page 9, ©PathDoc/ Shutterstock; page 10, ©Claudia Paulussen/Shutterstock; page 11, ©Rob Byron/Shutterstock; page 12, ©DavidPinoPhotography/Shutterstock; page 13, ©Ferenc Szelepcsenyi/Shutterstock; pages 14 and 27 ©Monkey Business Images/Shutterstock; page 16, ©Pavel L Photo and Video/Shutterstock; page 17, ©Sergio Schnitzler; page 18, ©Jesse Kunerth; page 19, ©Braam Collins; page 20, ©Oksana Kuzmina; page 21, ©Pixeljoy/Shutterstock; page 22, ©Everything/Shutterstock; page 23, ©Coprid/Shutterstock; page 24, ©trekandshoot/Shutterstock; page 25, ©Mike Tan/Shutterstock; page 26, ©Gordana Sermek/ Shutterstock; page 28, ©FashionStock.com/Shutterstock; page 29, ©karelnoppe/Shutterstock

LIBRARY OF CONGRESS CATALOGING-IN-PUBLICATION DATA
Orr, Tamra, author.
  Understanding sound / by Tamra B. Orr.
    pages cm — (Science explorer) (Follow the clues)
  Includes bibliographical references and index.
  Audience: 4 to 6.
  ISBN 978-1-63362-393-4 (lib. bdg.) — ISBN 978-1-63362-449-8 (pdf) —
ISBN 978-1-63362-421-4 (pbk.) — ISBN 978-1-63362-477-1 (e-book)
  1. Sound—Juvenile literature. I. Title. II. Series: Science explorer. III.
Series: Orr, Tamra. Follow the clues.

QC225.5.O77 2015
  534—dc23   2015006924

Cherry Lake Publishing would like to acknowledge
the work of the Partnership for 21st Century Skills.
Please visit www.p21.org for more information.

Printed in the United States of America, Corporate Graphics
July 2015

TABLE OF CONTENTS

CHAPTER 1

SCHOOL'S GOT TALENT

Assembling a stage takes a lot of hard work.

"Henry, steady the ladder for me, please," Marshall asked as he stepped up on the bottom rung.

"Be careful," Lilly cautioned, watching her two best friends attempting to secure a painted backdrop to the stage.

When Mr. Hooper had first announced that the school was going to hold a talent show in the cafeteria, Lilly had panicked. She didn't sing, dance, act, or do magic tricks. She was great at doing complex math

problems in her head, but that skill did not play well in front of an audience. Marshall and Henry had felt the same way. They wanted to be part of the talent show, but they didn't have anything to show off.

Mr. Hooper had helped them find the perfect solution. He needed a team to work behind the scenes. They would paint backdrops, hang lights, and run errands. Lilly, Marshall, and Henry volunteered immediately. Being part of the show without being in the spotlight was exactly what they wanted. So far, it had been great fun.

The only person who did not seem to be having much fun was Mr. Hooper. He looked frustrated.

"I absolutely cannot get the sound right in this room," he told the kids. "Every time I test it, the sound is muddled. That is going to be a

Many of the kids at school were practicing their talents to get ready for the show.

real problem when students perform. Only the people in the front tables will be able to hear them clearly."

"What are you going to do?" Henry asked.

"I am calling in an expert," Mr. Hooper replied. "A friend of mine from years back happens to be an expert in **acoustics**. I am going to ask her to help us figure out why the sound is bouncing around so much."

"The sound is bouncing?" asked Marshall. "What does that mean?"

"Sound is an invisible form of energy," Mr. Hooper explained. "It is made by vibrations. Put your hand on your throat while you talk. Do you feel the vibrations the sound is making?"

Henry, Lilly, and Marshall tried it. Mr. Hooper was right.

Sounds are waves. They can travel along a string that is pulled taut, which is how a tin can telephone works.

"Now think of a rubber band. If you stretch it between your fingers and pull down on one side, it makes a sound as it snaps back into place. This sound comes from the vibrations the rubber band is sending out. The vibrations can travel through a variety of mediums, such as air or water. These are sound waves."

"Does the sound fade as it travels?" Lilly asked. "When I throw a rock into water, it ripples out. As the ripples travel, they get smaller and smaller until they disappear."

A guitar produces sound when its strings vibrate.

"Water ripples and sound waves are different, but you've got the right idea," Mr. Hooper answered. "How far a sound wave travels depends largely on what it runs into on the way and what kind of material it is traveling through. Sometimes a sound wave reflects off of an object or is scattered. Sometimes it travels straight through something, and sometimes it is absorbed." He paused and pulled out his phone to check the time. "You three head back to the classroom, and I will meet you there to demonstrate what I mean about sound waves. Right now, I have to call my friend to see if she can come by the school tomorrow. I know she will be able to help us figure out why we have such terrible sound in here and what we can do about it."

EXAMINING AN EAR

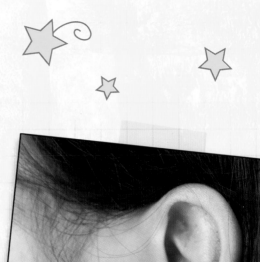

Ears are shaped to catch sound waves and reflect them into your head.

Have you ever taken a close look at your ear? If you have, you might realize why it is so good at helping you hear. It curls around to capture sound waves and funnels them right to your eardrum. The skin on your eardrum works a lot like the head of a regular drum. When sound waves hit it, it begins to vibrate. The vibration keeps going to three tiny bones called the hammer, anvil, and stirrup. These are the smallest bones in your entire body.

Next, the vibrations move to a membrane. This makes the fluid inside the inner ear vibrate. Thousands of tiny hair cells detect different sounds and send electrical signals to the brain. This is how you finally hear the sound. Amazing!

CHAPTER 2

BOUNCED AND SCATTERED

↰ Why do you think some sounds are harder to hear than others?

Mr. Hooper had a big smile on his face as he walked into the classroom. "Katherine, my friend, will stop by tomorrow after school," he said. "I'm sure she will have some great ideas. Now let's go back to what I was talking about before."

He picked up a large textbook and a stuffed duck named Dazzle that was kept in the corner as a mascot. "Sit down over here, Lilly," he said. Lilly pulled out a chair and sat down at the table. Mr. Hooper held the book in front of her face. "Marshall, stand over by the wall," he instructed.

Covering your ears makes things quieter, but some sound waves will probably still make it past your hands.

"Now start talking, Lilly," Mr. Hooper said.

Lilly began chatting about the book she was reading.

"Pay attention to how well you can hear her, Marshall," said Mr. Hooper. Then he moved the book and held Dazzle in front of Lilly's face. "Start talking again," he said. She did, and Marshall listened carefully.

"Okay, Marshall," said Mr. Hooper. "Tell us what you heard."

"It was more about what I didn't hear," replied Marshall. "When the book was there, I could hear her voice but it seemed to be a long way away, like it was being blocked. When you put the duck there though, it was like she was muffled. The volume went down."

"Right," Mr. Hooper agreed. "When sound waves hit something hard and slippery like the cover of a textbook, they are reflected. On the other hand,

when sound waves hit something soft like Dazzle, the waves are mostly absorbed. The rest pass through the duck and continue through the air."

"That makes sense," said Henry, "but why are we worrying about ducks? I am pretty sure there aren't any stuffed animals in the cafeteria to work around."

Everyone laughed. "No, there aren't any ducks," Mr. Hooper admitted, "but there are a number of hard materials there. Can you think of items that might reflect sound in the cafeteria?"

"The tables?" Lilly suggested.

"And the chairs," Marshall added.

"Wait a minute," Henry interrupted. "You also said sound waves can scatter. How does that happen?"

 A typical cafeteria is filled with objects that can reflect, scatter, or absorb sounds.

"Oh, I'm glad you reminded me," said Mr. Hooper. "If you have hard and smooth objects that have uneven surfaces, the sound waves tend to scatter or **diffuse**."

"Can you give us an example?" Lilly asked.

"How about rows of books that are different heights and widths?" Mr. Hooper suggested. "Sound waves would bounce between the surfaces in different directions until they are reflected in a direction where they do not hit the books again."

"Considering what's in the cafeteria then, I would guess that sounds are bouncing too much," Henry said thoughtfully. "That is why it's hard to hear clearly beyond those first tables."

"And that is why we hope to get some helpful answers from Katherine tomorrow," added Mr. Hooper.

Because books come in many sizes and shapes, full shelves can reflect sounds in all different directions.

STUDYING SOUND

Acoustical engineers might help design a room to make music sound especially loud and clear.

Acoustics is the study of sound. An acoustical engineer is a person whose job is to understand how sound works and how to manipulate it. Within this field, there are many different specialties that engineers can pursue.

An architectural acoustical engineer focuses on the sound within buildings, from houses and classrooms to concert halls and factories. Other acoustical engineers center on speech and hearing, underwater noise, medical acoustics, and noise control.

If you are interested in becoming an acoustical engineer, you will need at least a bachelor's degree in engineering, math, architecture, or physics. This will likely be followed by a master's degree in acoustics or mechanical engineering. Most engineers must also take at least one licensing exam after finishing college.

CHAPTER 3

THAT'S WHAT FRIENDS ARE FOR

With so many people talking, laughing, and eating, a cafeteria can be a very noisy place.

The next afternoon, Lilly, Marshall, and Henry headed straight to the cafeteria after school. Mr. Hooper was already in deep conversation with a tall woman with red hair.

"I'm glad you're here," Mr. Hooper said as he turned to greet his students. "This is my old friend Katherine Thomas. Katherine, this is my great backstage team."

After shaking their hands, Katherine stood in the middle of the cafeteria and looked around. "Your main problem," she said to them, "is that you are trying to combine your auditorium with your cafeteria."

"Why is that a problem, Ms. Thomas?" asked Lilly.

"It actually saved the school a great deal of money and space," Mr. Hooper said.

"Definitely," Katherine agreed. "However, a cafeteria is not designed with performances in mind. Think about what it sounds like when you're standing in the cafeteria during a lunch period. All sorts of different sounds are bouncing around. You hear a mix of people talking, dishes clanking together, and much more. It is hard to pick a single sound out of the jumble of noises. And if the cafeteria was empty, you probably wouldn't be able to hear very well if someone was talking to you from across the room."

The kids nodded. That made sense.

"An auditorium is different," Katherine continued. "It is built to maximize sound from a single location—the stage. Auditorium designers want to increase the sound of what is going on onstage, but decrease the noise of people talking in the audience, doors opening and closing, and so on."

"Oh!" Marshall exclaimed. "In other words, a cafeteria and an auditorium were built for not only different activities but also different ways of dealing with noise."

"Exactly," said Katherine. "The shapes of these rooms, the materials used to build them, and other factors all play a role in how they cause sounds to behave."

"But we don't have the time to build a whole new room for the talent show," said Lilly.

"Or the money," Mr. Hooper added.

"Of course not," Katherine said. "That is where variable acoustics come in." There was a puzzled silence, and then she grinned. "What does that term mean? Good question." She pulled a photo album out of her messenger bag and opened it on one of the cafeteria tables. "These are some examples of ways to improve the sound quality in large rooms like your cafeteria. What do you see?"

Mr. Hooper leaned over to flip some of the pages. "Oh," he said quietly. "I get it."

An auditorium is designed to project sound out to the audience.

Acoustical panels
are a common sight
in recording studios,
auditoriums, and other
places where sound
quality is important.
They are made of
soft materials and are
shaped to absorb as
much sound as possible.

Lilly, Marshall, and Henry looked at the pictures.

"What are these?" Marshall asked, pointing to a series of squares and rectangles hung on the walls in the photos.

"Those are acoustical panels," Katherine explained. "You hang them on walls or ceilings, and they absorb sound. This means you can make sound waves go where you want instead of letting them bounce all over the place. Right now, when someone sings or speaks from your stage area, that person's voice bounces back and forth all over the room. Some of the audience members will hear the same sound waves reflected from different directions. This makes the sound hard to understand. Hanging these panels would make a great difference in your sound quality."

Acoustical panels are often hung from the ceiling in theaters and auditoriums.

"Where are we going to find these panels before the talent show next week?" Marshall asked.

Mr. Hooper frowned. "Good question."

Katherine shook her head. "If we had more time, I could show you how to build your own. They are fairly simple and inexpensive. Don't worry, though. We have some extras at the university where I work. You can borrow them for the show. I will even come over and help you figure out where to put them. I think they will make a big difference."

"Wow," said Lilly. "You should win first prize in the talent show for all this help, Ms. Thomas!"

"As long as I don't have to sing, dance, or act, I'm in," laughed Katherine.

CAN YOU WIGGLE?

Animals such as deer can rotate their ears to focus on sounds coming from specific locations.

Have you ever noticed that some animals have huge ears? The bigger an animal's ears are, the easier it is for them to collect sound waves from the air. Elephants have the largest ears of all. They can hear extremely low sounds coming from more than 5 miles (8 kilometers) away.

Some animals can move their ears in a variety of positions. This allows them to focus on sounds coming from different directions. Take a look at videos of horses, rabbits, and kangaroos. Watch how their ears change when they hear a sound. The muscles these animals use to shift their ears are found in humans, too. However, they are usually inactive. Are yours? Check if you can wiggle or move your ears at all. If you can, those muscles are the reason why!

CHAPTER 4

TIME TO EXPERIMENT

↶ The Internet is a great place to start when you're looking for ways to solve a problem.

Henry burst into the cafeteria the next day and ran to find Mr. Hooper. "I thought of something else we could do to help prevent sound from bouncing around in the cafeteria," he said. "Can we do an experiment and try it out?"

Mr. Hooper smiled. "Sure," he said. "Go get Marshall and Lilly and meet me in the classroom. We can use the scientific method to see if your plan will work."

Like acoustical panels, rugs can absorb sound waves.

STEPS OF THE SCIENTIFIC METHOD
Step 1: Ask the question.
Step 2: Do background research.
Step 3: Form a **hypothesis**.
Step 4: Test the hypothesis.
Step 5: Analyze data and draw conclusions.
Step 6: Communicate results.

Once everyone was gathered in the classroom, Henry began telling them about his idea. "I went online last night and looked up all kinds of articles about how to improve the sound quality in a room," he explained. "I thought we could try a few of the suggestions in our classroom and see how it affects the noise levels. For example, why not put tablecloths on all of the tables? We could put some rugs on the floor, too. My hypothesis is that these things will work the same way as acoustical panels."

"Great minds really do think alike," Mr. Hooper agreed. "I happened to bring some rugs with me! First, let's walk around and talk for a few minutes. I want you to pay close attention to the level of sound."

Lilly, Marshall, and Henry did as Mr. Hooper asked. They were all surprised at how loud even the smallest noises were when they paid extra attention.

"Now, let's make some changes in here," said Mr. Hooper. He unrolled three rugs, and the kids moved desks so that he could spread each one out on the floor. Again, they walked around and talked, listening to how the sound changed. Next, Mr. Hooper closed the curtains, and they repeated the process. Finally, he hung up a United States flag in one corner and a state flag in another corner.

"One more time," Mr. Hooper instructed. "Walk around and make noise like you did before. Notice the difference."

"That is amazing," Marshall said. "It is so much quieter in here."

"The rugs, curtains, and flags absorbed the sound waves, right?" Lilly asked.

When it comes to sound waves, the glass of a window is hard and reflective, but curtains are soft and absorbent.

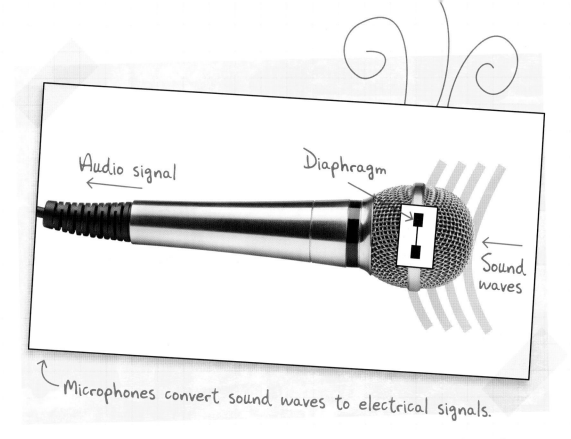

Audio signal

Diaphragm

Sound waves

Microphones convert sound waves to electrical signals.

"Yes, and that is how we will help reduce extra noise in the cafeteria at the talent show," Mr. Hooper agreed. "Now I have a new question for you. What can we do to increase the noise we do want to hear—the sound of the kids performing onstage?"

The kids thought for a moment. They had been concentrating so hard on how to **suppress** noise, they had forgotten they would have to **amplify** some of it.

"In a real auditorium, the shape of the room helps direct reflected sound waves out to the whole audience," Mr. Hooper explained. "Unfortunately, we don't have that option."

"The performers could yell really loud," Marshall suggested.

Mr. Hooper laughed. "True," he admitted. "But what else could they do?"

"They could use microphones," Henry suggested. Mr. Hooper nodded.

"How do microphones make everything louder, anyway?" Lilly asked.

An amplifier makes the sound louder, and speakers convert the electrical signal back to sound waves.

"Microphones are what are called transducers," Mr. Hooper explained. "Transducers convert energy from one form to another. As you learned, sound waves are a type of energy. Microphones convert these sound waves into electrical energy."

"How?" Marshall asked.

"The head of a microphone has a thin piece of paper, plastic, or metal inside called a **diaphragm**," Mr. Hooper replied. "When sound waves hit it, it vibrates. This causes other parts of the microphone to vibrate, and this is turned into an electrical signal. An amplifier and speakers use this signal to create a loud sound."

Just then, there was a knock on the door. Katherine stuck her head in and asked, "Ready to hang up some panels?"

Everyone hopped up. It was time to get to work.

TOO MANY DECIBELS

The jet engines of an airplane can be extremely loud

The amplitude of a sound is measured in a unit called a decibel. A normal conversation between a few people runs about 60 decibels (dB), while a crying baby might reach 110 dB. Sounds that measure more than 120 dB can be physically painful to hear. At 180 dB, hearing damage is caused almost immediately.

Here are some examples of common sounds and their decibel measurements.

Faint (30 dB or less): whisper in a quiet library; soft breeze

Moderate (40 to 60 dB): moderate rainfall; dishwasher; clothes dryer

Very Loud (70 to 90 dB): vacuum cleaner; blow dryer; alarm clock; kitchen blender; food processor

Extremely Loud (90 to 110 dB): passing motorcycle; hand drill; snowblower; gas lawn mower; chainsaw

Painful (115 to 165 dB): jet plane takeoff; ambulance siren; jackhammer; loud rock concert; fireworks at close distance

CHAPTER 5

BRAVO!

The show featured performances from dancers, musicians, singers, actors, and others.

"Henry, get ready to close the curtains on my signal," Lilly whispered. "Marshall, are you ready to move the spotlight?"

The talent show was almost over. The three friends had done their jobs perfectly, and Mr. Hooper had a smile that seemed to reach from ear to ear. Large rugs were spread out on the cafeteria floor, and borrowed acoustical panels hung on the walls.

Jennifer Cooper finished her tap dance routine, and the curtains closed as she walked off the stage. For a moment, there was silence, and then the crowd burst into applause and cheers. The show had gone very well, other than Jacob Brown forgetting the last line of his speech, LaToya Johnson stumbling on her last cartwheel, and Maria Gomez getting stage fright at the last minute.

"Hey guys, gather round," Mr. Hooper said. "I want you to know that I did a little experimenting out there in the audience. I sat in the front and then in the middle. I even stood in the back for a little while. I could hear everything clearly from each spot."

"In other words, our hypothesis about improving the sound for the show was right, and our results proved our conclusion!" Lilly said.

Relatives, friends, and other audience members were thrilled with the show.

With the skills they learned, the three friends were certain that next year's show would be even better.

"Indeed," Mr. Hooper agreed.

All of their hard work hanging the acoustical panels, putting tablecloths on each of the tables, and setting up a sound system had turned the school's first talent show into a true success. Even Katherine had stayed to watch and was pleased with the acoustic results.

As the parents and students filed slowly out of the cafeteria, Principal Sparks waved at Mr. Hooper. "Great job tonight," she said, walking over and shaking his hand. "I think this talent show is going to become an annual event."

"Dibs on being back on the stage crew," Marshall whispered to his friends.

"We can call ourselves the Sound Wave Trio," Lilly said.

"Hey Ms. Thomas," Henry called out. "Tell us more about building those sound panels . . ."

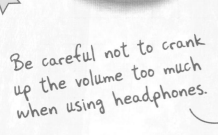

PROTECTING YOUR HEARING

Be careful not to crank up the volume too much when using headphones.

Remember those hair cells that are found in your inner ear? You are born with 15,000 to 20,000 of them. If any of them die, they cannot be regrown or replaced. Can you guess what happens if enough of them die? Your ability to hear slowly fades away.

Brief, intense sounds can permanently damage the ears. Standing too close as a firecracker goes off would be one example of this. Continuous exposure to slightly lower levels of noise can also destroy hair cells. For example, you can damage your hearing by listening to music too loud on headphones. You probably won't notice any hearing loss at first. But one day, you may not be able to hear your favorite music nearly as well as you do now. Protect those hair cells!

GLOSSARY

acoustics (uh-KOO-stiks) the study of sound

amplify (AM-pli-fye) to make something louder or stronger

amplitude (AM-pli-tood) the size of the vibrations in a sound wave; sounds with higher amplitudes are louder

decibel (DES-uh-buhl) a unit for measuring the loudness of sounds

diaphragm (DYE-uh-fram) a thin disc that vibrates when receiving or producing sound waves

diffuse (dif-YOOZ) to spread or scatter

eardrum (EER-druhm) a thin piece of skin inside the ear that vibrates when sound hits it, which makes us able to hear

hypothesis (hye-PAH-thi-sis) an idea that could explain how something works but that has to be tested through experiments to be proven right

membrane (MEM-brane) a very thin layer of tissue that lines or covers certain organs or cells

suppress (suh-PRESS) to hold back or control the expression of something

FOR MORE INFORMATION

BOOKS

Boothroyd, Jennifer. *Vibrations Make Sound*. Minneapolis: Lerner
    Publications, 2015.

Johnson, Robin. *What Are Sound Waves?* New York: Crabtree Publishing,
    2014.

Mahaney, Ian F. *Sound Waves*. New York: PowerKids Press, 2007.

Mara, Wil. *Sound Engineer*. Ann Arbor, MI: Cherry Lake Publishing, 2016.

WEB SITES

Kids Discover—Sound and Vibration

www.kidsdiscover.com/spotlight/sound-and-vibration/

Learn more about sound waves and hearing.

Science Kids at Home—What Is Sound?

www.sciencekidsathome.com/science_topics/what_is_sound.html

Find out how musical instruments create sound waves.

INDEX

ABOUT THE AUTHOR

Tamra Orr is an author living in the Pacific Northwest. Orr has a degree in secondary education and English from Ball State University. She is the mother to four and the author of hundreds of books for readers of all ages. When she isn't writing or reading books, she is writing letters to friends all over the world. Although fascinated by all aspects of science, most of her current scientific method skills are put to use tracking down lost socks, missing keys, and overdue library books.